# Cartooning

Deri Robins

QED Publishing

First published in the UK in 2004 by
QED Publishing
A Quarto Group Company
226 City Road
London, EC1V 2TT

www.qed-publishing.co.uk

A Catalogue record for this book is available
from the British Library.

ISBN 1 84538 277 3

Written by Deri Robins
Designed by Wladek Szechter/Louise Morley
Edited by Sian Morgan and Matthew Harvey

Creative Director: Louise Morley
Editorial Manager: Jean Coppendale

Picture credits
Corbis /Douglas Kirkland 6t /Jack Keely 8–9, 11, 14,
18–19, 20, 25/ Roger Armstrong 8; Don Jardine: 14 /
Ed Nofziger 17 /Jim Robins 17b

Printed and bound in China

The words in **bold** are
explained in the Glossary
on page 30.

# Contents

# Tools and materials

Anyone can draw cartoons – the more you practise, the better you'll become! This book has lots of ideas to help you improve your cartooning skills, along with projects to try out both at home and at school.

## Tools of the trade

All you really need is a pencil and plenty of paper, but it's also good to experiment with as many different materials as possible. **HB** or **B** pencils are ideal for first sketches – they rub out easily. You can go over the **outlines** in pen at the end.

## Cartoon experiments!

Why not try using some other cartooning tools? For example, marker pens are great for drawing big, bold cartoons. You can use felt tips, poster paints and inks for making bold, colourful cartoons and coloured inks and **watercolours** are good for soft colours. Remember, if you use paint or ink, draw your outlines in waterproof pen or they will run when you start painting.

## Paper

Use scrap paper for your rough ideas and smooth drawing paper for your finished cartoons.

There are lots of different materials you can use to create cartoons. As you experiment with different pens, paints and pencils, you'll see they all create different effects.

crayons

pastels

pencils

felt tips

## Drawing board

You need a hard surface to support your paper when you're drawing. Use a board positioned at a slight slope and keep the paper in place with masking tape or drawing pins. You need plenty of light when you are drawing, either from natural sunlight or a desk lamp.

## Protect your cartoons

Artwork is easily damaged. Tape your best pictures to a piece of card and tape a piece of coloured paper over the top to protect it.

**Keep your ideas in a notebook or sketchbook.**

**art paper**

**poster paint**

**coloured ink**

# Cartoon tips

Look for cartoon inspiration wherever you are: at home, at school, in the country or at the seaside. Draw a person, an animal or an object that you know well or use your imagination to create a fantasy character or monster.

## What is a cartoon?

What makes cartoons different from other drawings? Think about your favourite cartoon characters from films, television, comics or picture books.

**'The Simpsons', created by Matt Groening, is known the world over.**

## ANIMAL MAGIC

Look carefully at different animals and make sketches of them. Real animals may not keep still for long, so look at books, magazines or on the Internet. You could also watch wildlife programmes on television. You can even use a microscope to look at tiny insects.

# People pictures

Look carefully at your family, friends or favourite celebrity. Everyone has a unique **feature** that would make a great cartoon. Collect photos of people in different outfits, positions and poses. Look at them for ideas when you draw your cartoons.

MUM

DAD

# Cool cartoons

You can get different effects depending on which tools you use. Use a black pen or felt tip to **outline** and **shade** your cartoons. Felt tips create bold outlines and flat colour. Coloured inks give a softer effect. Combine a black ink outline with pencils, coloured ink or **watercolour**.

# Cartoon figures

The easiest way to draw a cartoon figure is to sketch a simple **outline** first and then add the details. You can start by drawing stick figures or round people. Try the cartoon figure below.

## Stick figures

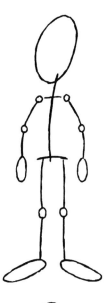

**1** Draw a stick figure and add an oval head, hands and feet. Put small circles at the joints.

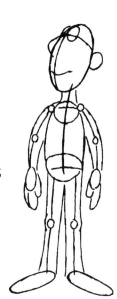

**3** Draw the **features** of the face and outlines of the body.

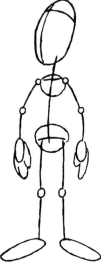

**2** Build up the figure by adding more ovals for the shoulders and hips.

**4** Finish by adding details for the face and clothing. Lastly, add colour to the cartoon.

## TIP

You can use circles and ovals to make cartoon figures: stretched ovals make tall, skinny figures, circles make plump people. Mix the two to create fat people with spindly legs.

**1** Draw the outline of your figure using circles and ovals.

**2** Now add details to make them funny, such as hair, clothes and shoes.

## Big and little

To draw a cartoon of somebody you know, look at them carefully. Are they tall or short? Fat or thin? Now exaggerate their most outstanding feature. Practise drawing from photographs.

# Faces and features

Faces and **expressions** are important in cartoons. The face is the part that people look at, so they should say a lot about the character. You can make them funny, angry, sad – or just silly.

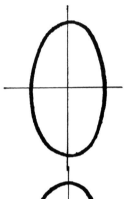

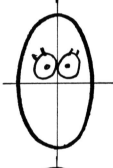

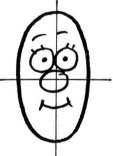

## Head on

**1** Draw an oval. Divide it into quarters.

**2** Put in the eyes just above the centre.

**3** Add the nose on the centre line. Add the mouth half way down.

**4** Add hair, eyebrows and eyelashes. Make your faces happy, sad or frightened.

## TIP

Try different face shapes: long and thin, short and fat! Fat heads have no neck. Thin heads look skinnier on a long, thin neck.

Hair can make a big difference to your characters. Different styles can make characters look scruffy or glamorous, young or old.

If you are making someone you know into a cartoon, look at them carefully. What do you notice most about them? Do they have a long chin? A wide face? Ears that stick out? A big nose? Glasses? These are the features you can exaggerate to make a great cartoon.

## TIP

Look at your reflection in the back of a large dessert spoon. With your face in the light against a dark **background**, draw what you see. Your face will be stretched and distorted. Copy this for an instant cartoon effect.

Remember glasses and jewellery. Details bring cartoons to life.

# Dressing up

The way you dress your cartoon characters helps to bring them to life. Clothes and hats can tell you where their owners live, what they do for a living or something about their personality.

## Mix-and-match book

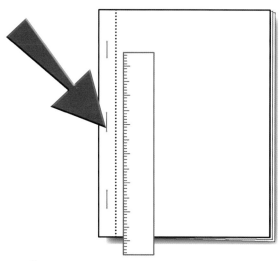

**1** Staple 6–8 sheets of unlined paper together to make a book. Draw a **vertical** line 5mm from the spine.

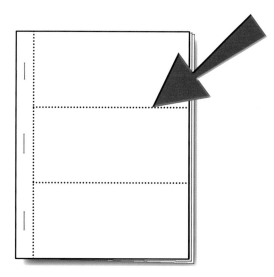

**2** On the first page, using the ruler, divide the page into three equal **horizontal** sections.

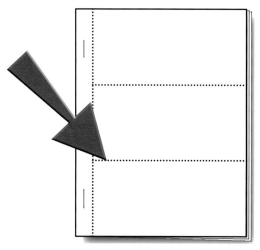

**3** Ask an adult for help with this step. Cut along the horizontal lines as far as the vertical line, using scissors.

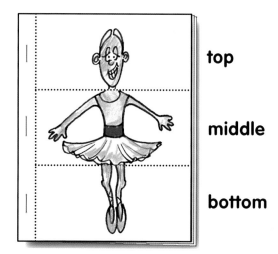

top

middle

bottom

**4** Draw a cartoon character on the first page. Put the head and neck in the top third, the body in the middle and the legs and feet in the bottom.

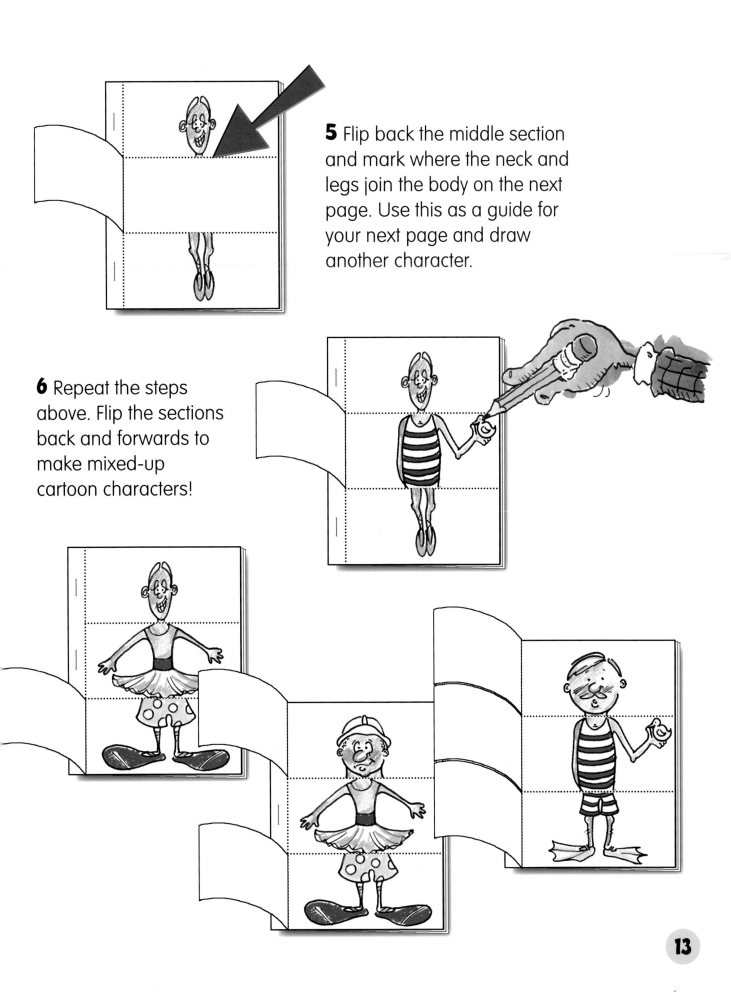

**5** Flip back the middle section and mark where the neck and legs join the body on the next page. Use this as a guide for your next page and draw another character.

**6** Repeat the steps above. Flip the sections back and forwards to make mixed-up cartoon characters!

# On the move

Now you've created your cartoon characters, you need to make them move. Follow the hints and tips below to get them running, jumping and flying.

## Action!

1    Begin with a simple stick figure.

2    Then add ovals and circles.

3    Now add clothes, colour and facial **expressions**.

**Jumping**

**Running**

Movement lines help to show which way something is moving – and how fast.

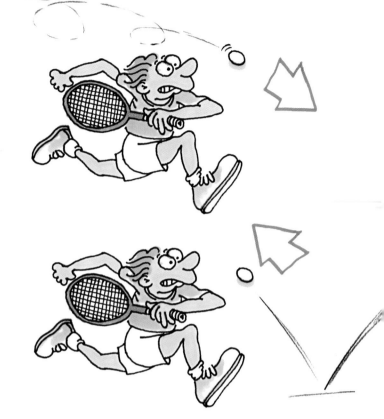

## TIP

Movement lines also add extra action to your cartoon – just look at the pictures below. Adding double movement lines behind these figures makes them look more active.

# Cartoon creatures

Before you start drawing cartoon animals, practise sketching real ones. Then try turning your sketches into cartoons.

## Drawing animals

Notice the **features** and **personalities** of a variety of animals. A dog's ears can be droopy or perky, depending on whether it is happy or sad.

## KOOKY ANIMALS

You can build up any kind of animal from simple shapes:

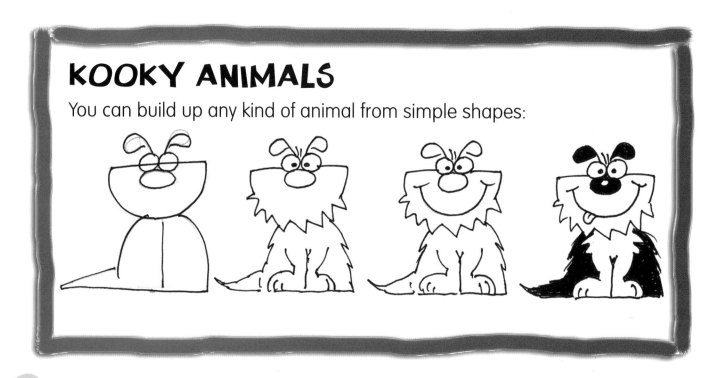

# Animal shapes

**1** Draw an **outline** of the head and body, using circles and ovals. Add the legs, feet and tail.

**2** Rub out the guide lines you don't want in the final picture.

**3** Use coloured pencils or pens to finish the drawing.

When you are confident about drawing animals, try stretching the body and limbs to make them taller and skinnier, or squash them for rounder, fatter, more comical cartoon creatures.

# PROJECT

**Create a new animal star**
Some animals have been turned into cartoons many times – especially bears and cats! Try to think of something more unusual and see what you can do with it. Will it be fierce or friendly? Clever or stupid? Fast or slow?

# It's alive!

Cartoons can make anything come to life. Look around your bedroom, garden or classroom for inspiration. You could turn your whole street into cartoon characters. The windows of the buildings could be the eyes and the doors could be mouths.

## Kitchen cartoons

Choose an object and get to know it well. Draw it so often, and from so many different angles, that it becomes as familiar as a friend.

Give it a name and turn its parts into human features: a spout or handle can become a nose, for example.

# Motor mouths

Give bikes, cars, scooters, skateboards, boats, trains and buses funny faces to bring them to life. Try to make the shapes match the expressions – for example, a car can be round, smiley and friendly, or long, low and aggressive, with a long radiator that looks like a mouthful of flashing teeth, and wicked eyes instead of headlights.

# Scary monsters

People, animals, buildings or houses can all make scary cartoons – and that's before you start drawing the real monsters, such as vampires, werewolves and ghosts!

Everyone will recognize a vampire. How about making up your own monsters?

Wicked witches are usually ugly and have pointed noses, long chins and warts on their faces.

**1**

**2**

**3**

You can make ghosts as black **silhouettes**, or as white, cloudy shapes with a soft, black **outline** in the shape of a whirlwind.

## MONSTER MIX UP

Try mixing parts of different animals into a new fantasy friend or **fiend**.

## A question of size

Even tiny creatures can become terrifying if they grow to a huge size.

## PROJECT

**Mythical monsters**

**Myths** and **legends** are full of strange and scary creatures, such as dragons, werewolves and devils. Choose a mythical monster and turn it into a cartoon. Will yours be scary, friendly or funny?

# Set the scene

Once you've created a group of cartoon characters, it's fun to put them in different **backgrounds**. Use real life or invent a fantasy world – your background will be far more interesting than a blank piece of paper.

## TIP

Always start by sketching your cartoon character in soft pencil first, and then add the background. Add **foreground** details last. When you are happy with the finished result, colour it in and go over the **outlines** in thick, black pen.

## Where to get ideas

Flick through travel magazines, photos and books, or look around your house, street or school – which of these scenes suit your cartoon characters? Draw some simple backgrounds – choose a few details that show where it is meant to be.

## Placing your character

Your character should appear to be part of the scene, not just stuck on top of it – make sure that there is some detail in front of it as well as behind.

## Night or day?

Night-time backgrounds are great for a spooky atmosphere. Draw your character and buildings in black **silhouette**.

# IN THE MOOD

Different skies set the mood, too. It's easy to fill the sky with snow or rain!

# Comic capers

Now that you've learned how to draw amazing cartoon figures, you can put them in your own comic story. First, take a look at some of your favourite comics. You'll see that the pages are split into **frames** of different sizes and shapes.

Frames don't have to be square! Try circles, ovals and ones with jagged edges. You can draw the frames by hand so that they are not all straight lines or draw them neatly with a ruler. Comic strips look more exciting if parts of the picture break out of the frame edges.

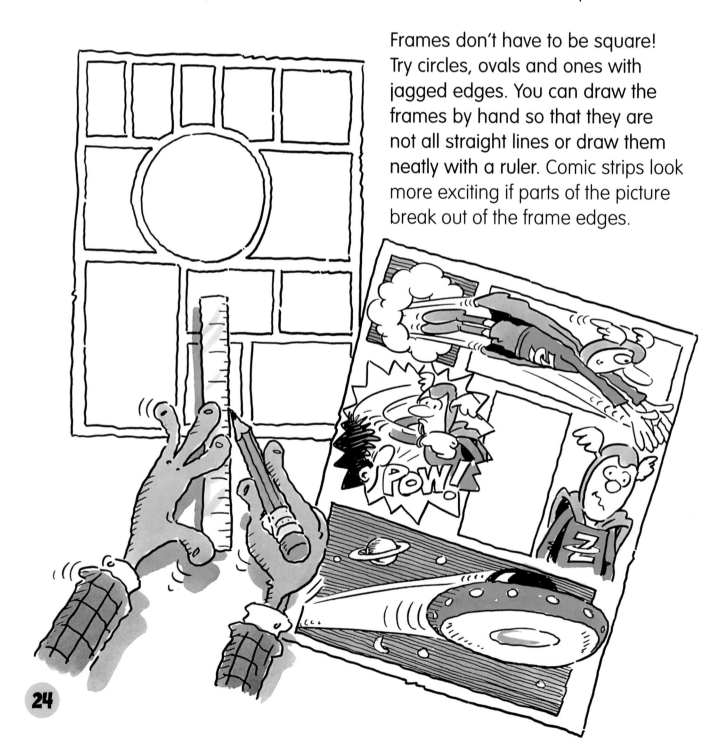

## Story lines

Your characters can 'talk' in speech and thought bubbles. You can put extra information in boxes at the top or bottom of the picture if you have left enough space. Speech bubbles are usually oval. Bubbles that look like clouds show a character's thoughts. Jagged bubbles show when someone is angry and shivery bubbles when they are scared.

## Exclamation marks!

Exclamation marks are used a lot in comics. To show people shouting, use a thick black marker pen.

## TIP

Speech and thought bubbles usually go in the top third of the picture, so draw your sketch in the bottom two-thirds.

# Make a comic

Now that you've seen how it's done, why not try creating your own comic story with your own cast of funny, scary or silly characters? You could even make a whole comic book.

## Lights, camera, action!

Making a comic strip is like making a film: you need a story, characters and a series of **backgrounds**. Start by thinking up a short, simple story with a beginning, a middle and an end. You could look through some joke books for a funny ending.

YOUR CARTOON **CHARACTER** CAN DO **ANYTHING!**

## Stars of the show

What will your main character look like? Decide what sort of **personality** they have and think of a name. Try drawing them from lots of different angles to get them right. You'll also need friends and enemies for the main character to talk to. Try not to have more than three characters, otherwise readers may get confused.

# Storyboarding

You're ready to make a storyboard. This is a rough sketch of each frame; it doesn't have to be neat. Try to vary the pictures. Sometimes characters can be in the distance, sometimes you can show a close-up of their face and **expression**.

# Comic frames

Once you are happy with your storyboard, turn it into a finished comic strip. Draw each box neatly, with a ruler and a pencil. Make sure you draw the frames big enough to fit all the details you want.

# Finishing off

Copy your drawings from the storyboard and turn them into finished cartoons. First, draw the **outlines** in pencil.

Go over the outlines in black marker pen or felt tip. Colour the pictures with paint or felt tips. Your comic is complete!

# Making movies

In an **animated** cartoon, thousands of pictures are shown at the rate of 24 pictures per second. This is too fast for our eyes, so we see a continual movement. If they were in an animated cartoon, these 12 pictures would appear on screen for just half a second.

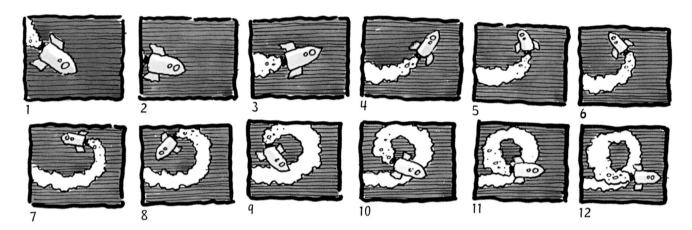

## Make a flick book

Make a simple flick book to see your cartoons really move! You will need a small, unlined notebook and a pen or pencil. Decide what you want to see animated – kicking a ball for instance. Think about what you do when you kick a ball – try it out and see what your arms and legs do.

**1** On a scrap of paper, from left to right, sketch about 20 stick figures. Change the position of the arms and legs slightly each time so that the figure really looks as if it is walking or kicking a ball.

**2** Copy the first stick figure in the bottom corner of the first page.

**3** Draw the second figure in the same place on the bottom corner of the next page. Keep going until you have drawn all the figures.

**4** Bend the book slightly with your thumb at the edge and let the pages flick up. Your figure will appear to move! This is similar to how cartoon films are made.

Try drawing different types of movement. Ask a friend to do the movements for you to copy or draw from your own reflection.

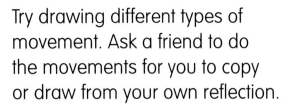

## TIP

Animators use 'key drawings' to help them work out a sequence of movements. If you want to draw someone running, jumping – or just drinking a cup of tea – draw the start, middle and end positions first. These are your 'key drawings' – all you need to do now is to draw the bits in between.

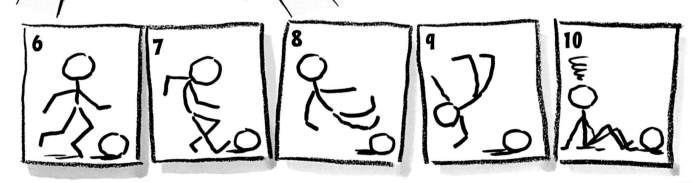

# Glossary

**animated**   images made to move by flashing lots of frames per second

**B**   soft pencil; even softer ones are marked 2B, 3B etc., up to 6B

**background**   things in the back of a picture, behind the main object

**expressions**   look on a person's face when they are happy, sad, puzzled, angry etc.

**features**   ears, nose, eyes and other parts of the face that make us all look different

**fiend**   an evil creature

**foreground**   area at the front of a picture

**frames**   boxes that make up a page in a comic book

**HB**   medium pencil, harder pencils are marked 2H, 3H etc., to 6H

**horizontal**   across the page

**legends**   stories about the past

**myths**   stories about superhuman beings in the past

**outline**   outer edge of something

**personality**   way a person behaves

**shade**   to add dark areas to a picture

**silhouette**   object with just its outline visible and filled with a colour

**vertical**   up and down the page

**watercolours**   paints that mix with water

# Index

# Notes for teachers

The cartoon projects in this book are aimed at children at Key Stage 2. They can be used as stand-alone projects or as a part of other areas of study. While the ideas in the book are offered as inspiration, children should always be encouraged to draw from their imagination and first-hand observation.

## Sourcing ideas

Whenever possible, art projects should tap into children's interests and be relevant to their lives and experiences. Try using stimulating starting points, such as friends, family or pets, holidays, hobbies, television programmes or topical events.

Encourage children to source their own ideas and references from comics, books, magazines, the Internet or CD-ROM collections.

If you have access to a camcorder, ask the children to storyboard a simple animated cartoon sequence and video it frame by frame to see how well it works. Encourage the children to think of music and sound effects to go with their cartoon, as well as ways of making the instruments from everyday objects.

Cartoon images can also be created from other media, such as clay or Plasticine. These can also be made into cartoons by using a video camera, changing the models each time you video a frame.

Use digital cameras to create reference material (landscapes, people or animals) and use it alongside the children's work (see below). Other lessons can often be an ideal springboard for a cartooning project – for example, a school trip or a story from Greek mythology could be retold in picture-strip form. Get the children to look at the way that picture-book illustrators such as Marcia Williams have used cartoon strips to retell history, legends and stories from literature.

Encourage children to keep a sketchbook to record their ideas, and to collect other images and objects to help them develop their cartoons.

Show Children a variety of animated cartoons, ranging from traditional and contemporary hand-drawn cartoons to computer-animated films and the clay-model cartoons of Aardman Animations. They can also look at a range of comic books, from simple comics aimed at toddlers to graphic novels.

## Evaluating work

Children should share their work with others, and compare ideas and methods – this is often very motivating. Encourage them to talk about their work. How would they do it differently next time? What do they like best/least about the work?

Help children to judge the originality and value of their work, to appreciate the different qualities in others' work and different ways of working. Display all the children's work.

Discuss the use of different materials, such as felt tips, markers, inks and watercolours. Experiment with different effects.

## Going further

Look at ways to develop projects – for example, adapt the cartoons to make printed T-shirts, cards and badges, or characters for board games. Use image-enhancing computer software and digital scanners to enhance, build up and juxtapose images in interesting and funny ways.

Work on a school comic, with a letters page, jokes and competitions. Parents and children could pay a small amount to advertise in the comic.

Set up and develop a class cartoon gallery on your school website.

# Learn ART

# Cartooning

Pick up a pencil and don't forget your crayons for this art class with a difference.

**From sketching outline figures to creating your own comic strips, this book will teach you all you need to know to become a crazy cartoonist. Draw cartoons of your family, create weird and wonderful monsters or even make a pig fly – with cartooning the only limit is your imagination!**

- **Packed with fun projects and imaginative ideas.**
- **Easy-to-follow instructions supported by step-by-step photographs.**
- **Teaches basic skills and techniques.**

**Other titles in this series:**
World Art
Stencils and Prints
Drawing and Sketching
Special Effects
Painting

£5.99     www.qed-publishing.co.uk

ISBN 1-84538-277-3

9 781845 382773

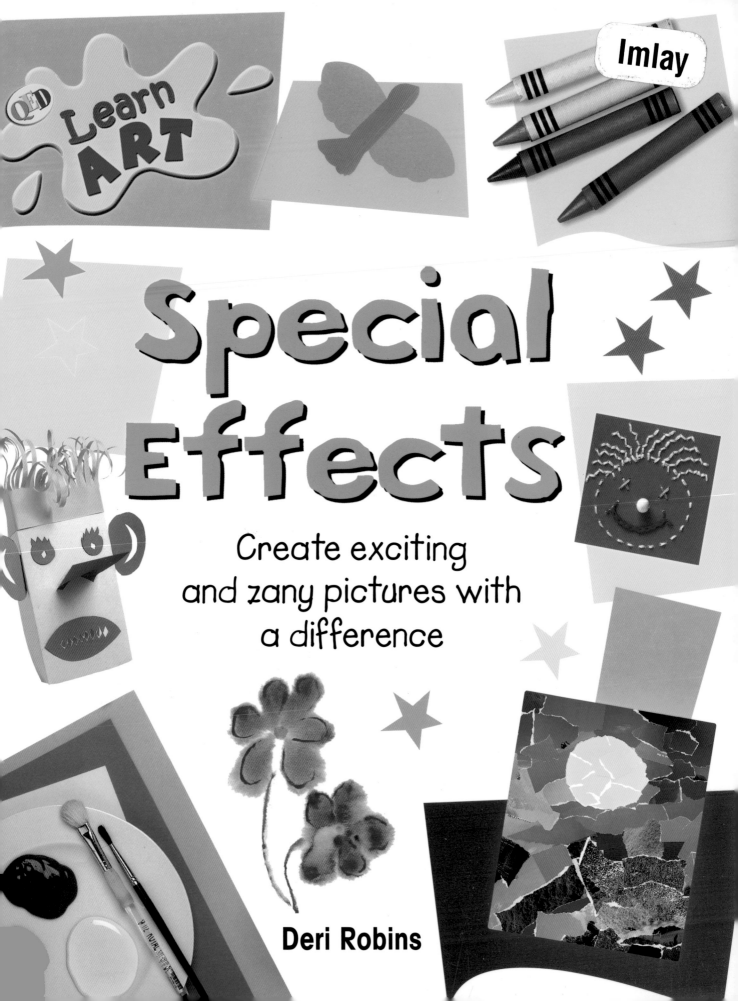

QED Learn ART

# Special Effects

## Create exciting and zany pictures with a difference

**Deri Robins**